Civil War Remembered

19 Quilts Using Reproduction Fabrics

Mary Etherington and Connie Tesene

Martingale
Create with Confidence

Civil War Remembered:
19 Quilts Using Reproduction Fabrics
© 2015 by Mary Etherington and Connie Tesene

Martingale®
19021 120th Ave. NE, Ste. 102
Bothell, WA 98011-9511 USA
ShopMartingale.com

Printed in China
20 19 18 17 16 15   8 7 6 5 4 3 2 1

Library of Congress Cataloging-in-Publication Data is available upon request.

ISBN: 978-1-60468-646-3

Mission Statement
Dedicated to providing quality products
and service to inspire creativity.

Credits

PUBLISHER AND CHIEF VISIONARY OFFICER
Jennifer Erbe Keltner

EDITOR IN CHIEF
Karen Costello Soltys

DESIGN DIRECTOR
Paula Schlosser

ACQUISITIONS EDITOR
Karen M. Burns

PHOTOGRAPHER
Brent Kane

TECHNICAL EDITOR
Nancy Mahoney

COVER AND
INTERIOR DESIGNER
Regina Girard

COPY EDITOR
Melissa Bryan

ILLUSTRATOR
Anne Moscicki

Contents

Introduction

I am feeling quite guilty having my name on this beautiful book. With the exception of the two little quilts called "Scorched," my partner of nearly 32 years has made every single quilt! And they are all special! Years ago I questioned Connie's use of red and orange together. Thank goodness I never spoke this out loud because over the years Connie has taught me everything about color and combining fabrics. When you look at these quilts you will begin to understand Connie's unique talent. As you pull fabrics from your own collection to make your own quilt, do not be surprised if the combination looks unusual.

Mary Ellen Hopkins once made a statement that we have always remembered, "You just cannot LOVE every single fabric in your quilt—you'll be too bored with it!" And she was right. If you have some odd ducks in your fabric collection, try throwing one in here and there in your quilt. Connie is known as someone who would not make a four-fabric quilt if her life depended on it! Many times she only has one triangle from a piece of fabric, and there are likely hundreds of different fabrics in each quilt.

Many years ago I copied a quilt by our friends at Little Quilts, and I searched for the exact fabrics that they used. I probably had every single one of them, and that quilt was fun in its own way. And yes, it looks just like the picture! But be brave and creative and adventurous when you make one of Connie's Civil War quilts. Remember what Bonnie Hunter says, "If you still hate a piece of fabric, you haven't cut it small enough yet!"

When this book reaches you, Country Threads Quilt Shop will have already been closed six months. Connie and I did not retire completely but we did close our retail shop November 1, 2014. We opened the shop in 1987, and since that time I had "company" at my house nearly six days a week. The quilt shop was located on my 10 acres with many pets and farm animals, lots of flowers and gardens, as well as outbuildings and lawn to mow. Both Connie and I are in good health but we wanted to enjoy sewing, reading, pets, gardening, collecting, decorating, music, and our families without the burden of a retail quilt shop. We've enjoyed every year of our business, but hope to continue sewing, making quilts and designing for others in the future. We are still business partners as we have been for over 32 years—so that's why my name is on this book. Thanks, Connie!

~ Mary E.

Those were very nice words from Mary but I'll let you in on a little secret . . . every quilt in this beautiful book had some "extra help." Mary always had an answer for my questions on a different setting for each quilt, color choices on setting triangles, and borders that broke away from the same old boring strips. Mary loves antique quilts and has quite a collection of her own. This along with numerous quilt history books were great inspiration for me. Thanks, Mary!

~ Connie

Path of Freedom

Started during the Colonial period, most likely by Quakers, the Underground Railroad system helped shelter runaway slaves from the South and guide them on their journey to find freedom in the northern United States and Canada. As more slaves gained their freedom in the mid-1800s, many worked to help others achieve independence in the years leading up to the end of the Civil War and the abolition of slavery.

Quilt size: 36½" x 36½"

Finished blocks: 6" x 6"

Materials

Yardage is based on 42"-wide fabric.

⅓ yard *each* of 4 assorted red prints for Star blocks

⅓ yard *each* of 4 assorted light prints for Star blocks and Double X blocks

⅛ yard *each* of 4 assorted navy prints for Double X blocks

⅛ yard *each* of 4 assorted gold prints for Double X blocks

⅛ yard of cream print for Double X blocks

⅛ yard of white print for Star block centers

⅓ yard of blue print for binding

1¼ yards of fabric for backing

40" x 40" piece of batting

Cutting

Measurements include ¼"-wide seam allowances.

From *each* of the assorted red prints, cut:

2 strips, 2" x 42"; crosscut into 40 squares, 2" x 2" (160 total)

4 squares, 3½" x 3½" (16 total)

From *each of 3* light prints, cut:

1 strip, 3½" x 42"; crosscut into 20 rectangles, 2" x 3½" (60 total)

1 strip, 2" x 42"; crosscut into 20 squares, 2" x 2" (60 total)

1 strip, 2⅞" x 42"; crosscut into 12 squares, 2⅞" x 2⅞" (36 total). Cut the squares in half diagonally to yield 24 triangles (72 total).

From *1* of the light prints, cut:

1 strip, 3½" x 42"; crosscut into 20 rectangles, 2" x 3½"

1 strip, 2" x 42"; crosscut into 20 squares, 2" x 2"

From the white print, cut:

4 squares, 3½" x 3½"

From the cream print, cut:

1 strip, 2⅞" x 42"; crosscut into 12 squares, 2⅞" x 2⅞". Cut the squares in half diagonally to yield 24 triangles.

From *each* of the assorted navy prints, cut:

1 strip, 2⅞" x 42"; crosscut into 12 squares, 2⅞" x 2⅞" (48 total). Cut the squares in half diagonally to yield 24 triangles (96 total).

From *each* of the assorted gold prints, cut:

1 strip, 2⅞" x 42"; crosscut into 12 squares, 2⅞" x 2⅞" (48 total). Cut the squares in half diagonally to yield 24 triangles (96 total).

From the blue print, cut:

4 strips, 2¼" x 42"

Making the Star Blocks

Use one light and one red print for each block.

1. Draw a diagonal line on the wrong side of each red 2" square. Place a marked square on a light rectangle, right sides together. Sew on the drawn line. Trim the outside corner of the red square only, ¼" from the stitched line. Press the seam allowances toward the corner. Repeat on the other end of the rectangle. Make four units.

Make 4.

2. Lay out the units from step 1, four light 2" squares, and one red 3½" square in three rows. Press the seam allowances as indicated. Join the rows and press. The block should measure 6½" x 6½". Make 16 blocks.

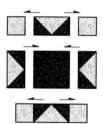

Make 16.

3. Referring to steps 1 and 2, make four blocks using one light print, one red print, and the white squares as shown.

Make 4.

Making the Double X Blocks

Use one light (or cream), one navy, and one gold print for each block.

1. Sew a light triangle to a navy triangle to make a half-square-triangle unit. Press the seam allowances toward the navy triangle. Make three units.

Make 3.

2. Sew a light triangle to a gold triangle to make a half-square-triangle unit. Press the seam allowances toward the gold triangle. Make three units.

Make 3.

3. Sew a gold triangle to a navy triangle to make a half-square-triangle unit. Press the seam allowances toward the navy triangle. Make three units.

Make 3.

4. Join the units from steps 1–3 into rows. Press the seam allowances as indicated. Join the rows and press the seam allowances toward the center. The block should measure 6½" x 6½". Make 16 blocks.

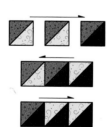

Make 16.

Assembling and Finishing the Quilt

1. Arrange the blocks in six rows of six blocks each, alternating the block designs and rotating the Double X blocks to form a gold diamond pattern in the quilt center as shown in the quilt-assembly diagram below.

2. Sew the blocks together into rows, pressing the seam allowances in opposite directions from row to row. Join the rows. Press the seam allowances in one direction.

Quilt assembly

3. Layer the backing, batting, and quilt top. Baste, and then quilt as desired.

4. Using the blue 2¼"-wide strips, make and attach binding.

Road to Victory

This quilt is full of surprises, with secondary hourglass and star elements forming where the flying geese come together. It involves a lot of piecing, so it's not for the faint of heart. But then, neither was the road to victory in any Civil War battle.

Quilt size: 47¾" x 59"

Finished blocks: 8" x 8"

Materials

Yardage is based on 42"-wide fabric.

2½ yards *total* of assorted light prints for blocks

1½ yards *total* of assorted dark prints in blue, gray, navy, and black for blocks

⅛ yard *each* of 10 to 12 assorted medium and medium-dark prints for flying-geese units*

1¼ yards of medium-red print for setting triangles

1 yard *total* of assorted red prints for blocks

½ yard of dark-red print for binding

3 yards of fabric for backing (pieced horizontally)

52" x 63" piece of batting

We used scraps in gold, teal, pink, orange, navy, black, red, gray, and blue.

Cutting

Measurements include ¼"-wide seam allowances.

From the assorted light prints, cut:

24 strips, 1½" x 42"; crosscut into 384 rectangles, 1½" x 2½"

7 strips, 3⅞" x 42"; crosscut into 64 squares, 3⅞" x 3⅞". Cut the squares in half diagonally to yield 128 triangles.

From the assorted medium and medium-dark prints, cut:

768 squares, 1½" x 1½"

From the assorted red prints, cut:

12 sets of 2 matching squares, 3⅞" x 3⅞" (24 total); cut the squares in half diagonally to yield 4 matching triangles (48 total)

12 squares, 2½" x 2½"

From the assorted dark prints, cut:

20 sets of 2 matching squares, 3⅞" x 3⅞" (40 total); cut the squares in half diagonally to yield 4 matching triangles (80 total)

20 squares, 2½" x 2½"

From the medium-red print, cut:

4 squares, 14¼" x 14¼"; cut the squares into quarters diagonally to yield 16 side triangles (2 will be left over)*

2 squares, 11" x 11"; cut the squares in half diagonally to yield 4 corner triangles*

From the dark-red print, cut:

6 strips, 2¼" x 42"

The side and corner triangles are slightly oversized and will be trimmed later.

Making the Stepping Stones Blocks

All 32 blocks are assembled the same way; only the color placement changes. Use one dark (or red) print for each block.

1. Select a matching pair of 1½" medium or medium-dark squares. Draw a diagonal line on the wrong side of each square. Place a marked square on a light rectangle, right sides together. Sew on the drawn line. Trim the outside corner of the medium or medium-dark square only, ¼" from the stitched line. Press the seam allowances toward the corner. Repeat on the other end of the rectangle. Make 12 units.

Make 12.

2. Randomly sew together three units from step 1 to make a flying-geese strip. Make sure all of the light triangles point in the same direction. Press the seam allowances in one direction. Make four strips.

Make 4.

3. Sew a light triangle to a dark triangle to make a half-square-triangle unit. Press the seam allowances toward the dark triangle. Make four units.

Make 4.

4. Lay out one dark 2½" square and the units from steps 2 and 3 in three rows. Join the units into rows and press the seam allowances as indicated. Join the rows and press the seam allowances in one direction. Make 12 blocks.

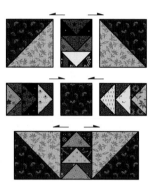

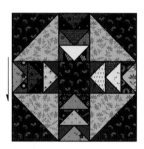

Make 20.

DISCOVERY

If you surround the center squares with four flying-geese units that have matching red triangles, a star will form in the center of the block. We didn't discover this until most of the blocks were made.

5. Referring to steps 1–4, make 20 blocks using one red print instead of a dark print for the 3⅞" triangles and center square.

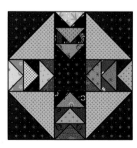

Make 12.

Assembling and Finishing the Quilt

1. Arrange the blocks and the medium-red side and corner triangles in diagonal rows, alternating the red and dark blocks and making sure to place dark blocks around the outer edges as shown in the quilt-assembly diagram below. Note that the red and dark blocks form a secondary hourglass pattern.

2. Join the blocks and side triangles into rows. Press the seam allowances as indicated. Join the rows and add the corner triangles last. Press the seam allowances as indicated. Trim the oversized triangles all around, leaving 1¼" from the block corners so that the quilt top measures 47¾" x 59".

3. Layer the backing, batting, and quilt top. Baste, and then quilt as desired.

4. Using the dark-red 2¼"-wide binding strips, make and attach binding.

Quilt assembly

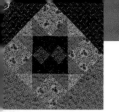

Battle for Glory

Stars have long been a symbol of victory and independence in the United States. Here, 30 stars with four-patch centers are set upon a field of double pink—a rich color that was popular in the late 1800s and that lends itself to both celebratory and somber themes. Here it represents the blood shed in the pursuit of glory on many a battlefield.

Quilt size: 51" x 59½"
Finished blocks: 6" x 6"

Materials

Yardage is based on 42"-wide fabric. Fat quarters are approximately 18" x 21".

1 fat quarter *each* of 24 assorted light prints for blocks
1⅔ yards of pink tone on tone for spacer blocks and border
¾ yard *total* of assorted dark prints for blocks*
⅔ yard of red print for setting triangles
½ yard *total* of assorted medium prints for blocks*
¼ yard *total* of assorted gold scraps for four-patch units
¼ yard *total* of assorted red scraps for four-patch units
½ yard of dark-brown print for bias binding
3¼ yards of fabric for backing (pieced horizontally)
55" x 64" piece of batting

We used scraps in gold, rust, red, brown, blue, teal, navy, and black.

Cutting

Measurements include ¼"-wide seam allowances.

From the assorted red scraps, cut:
30 sets of 2 matching squares, 1½" x 1½" (60 total)

From the assorted gold scraps, cut:
30 sets of 2 matching squares, 1½" x 1½" (60 total)

From the assorted dark prints, cut:
30 squares, 3¼" x 3¼"; cut the squares into quarters diagonally to yield 120 triangles

From the assorted medium prints, cut:
30 sets of 2 matching squares, 3¼" x 3¼" (60 total); cut the squares into quarters diagonally to yield 8 matching triangles (240 total)

From the assorted light prints, cut:
30 squares, 3¼" x 3¼"; cut the squares into quarters diagonally to yield 120 triangles
30 sets of 4 matching squares, 2½" x 2½" (120 total)

From the pink tone on tone, cut:
4 strips, 6½" x 42"; crosscut into 20 squares, 6½" x 6½"
6 strips, 4½" x 42"

From the red print, cut:
5 squares, 10" x 10"; cut the squares into quarters diagonally to yield 20 side triangles (2 will be left over)*
2 squares, 6" x 6"; cut the squares in half diagonally to yield 4 corner triangles*

From the dark-brown print, cut:
2¼"-wide bias strips, enough to yield 250" of binding

The side and corner triangles are slightly oversized and will be trimmed later.

Making the Star Blocks

Use one red, one gold, one medium, one dark, and two light prints for each block.

1. Sew two red and two gold 1½" squares together to make one four-patch unit as shown. Press the seam allowances as indicated.

Make 1.

2. Join one light, one dark, and two medium 3¼" triangles. Press the seam allowances as indicated. Make four matching units.

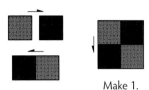

3. Sew the units from steps 1 and 2 together with four matching light 2½" squares. Press the seam allowances as indicated. The block should measure 6½" x 6½". Make 30 blocks.

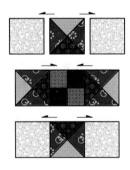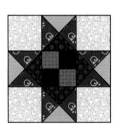

Make 30.

Assembling and Finishing the Quilt

1. Arrange the blocks, pink 6½" squares, and red side and corner triangles in diagonal rows as shown in the quilt-assembly diagram, upper right. Sew the blocks, squares, and side triangles into rows. Join the rows and add the corner triangles last. Press the seam allowances as indicated. Trim the oversized triangles all around, leaving an equal amount from the block corners so that the quilt top measures 43" x 51½".

Quilt assembly

2. Join the pink 4½"-wide strips end to end. From the pieced strip, cut two 43"-long strips and two 59½"-long strips. Sew the 43"-long strips to the top and bottom of the quilt top. Press the seam allowances toward the pink strips. Sew the 59½"-long strips to the sides of the quilt top. Press the seam allowances toward the pink strips.

3. Layer the backing, batting, and quilt top. Baste, and then quilt as desired.

4. You can leave the quilt top square, or round the corners as we did. Place a 5"-diameter plate or cardboard circle on the corner and trace the curve. Trim the corner on the drawn line.

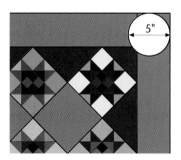

5. Using the dark-brown 2¼"-wide bias-binding strips, make and attach bias binding.

One Flag

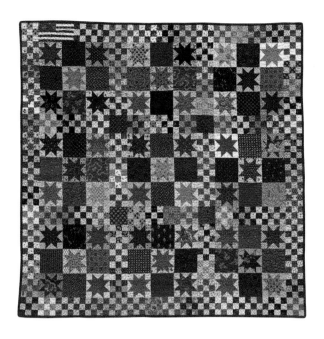

Quilt size: 36½" x 36½"

Finished blocks: 3" x 3", 2¼" x 2¼", and 2¼" x 4½"

Materials

Yardage is based on 42"-wide fabric. Fat quarters are approximately 18" x 21".

1 fat quarter *each* (or scraps) of 15 assorted medium or dark prints in black, navy, blue, teal, light blue, green, sour green, brown, red, pink, orange, gold, and rust for blocks and spacer squares

1 fat quarter *each* (or scraps) of 15 assorted light or medium-light prints for blocks

⅓ yard of dark-brown print for binding

1¼ yards of fabric for backing

40" x 40" piece of batting

Cutting

Measurements include ¼"-wide seam allowances.

Cutting for 1 Star Block

Cut 45 blocks total.

From *1* of the medium or dark prints, cut:
1 square, 2" x 2"
8 squares, 1¼" x 1¼"

From *1* of the light or medium-light prints, cut:
4 rectangles, 1¼" x 2"
4 squares, 1¼" x 1¼"

Cutting for Spacer Squares

From the assorted dark prints, cut:
36 squares, 3½" x 3½"

Cutting for 1 Nine Patch Block

Cut 53 blocks total.

From *1* of the dark prints, cut:
5 squares, 1¼" x 1¼"

From *1* of the light prints, cut:
4 squares, 1¼" x 1¼"

Don't let any bit of your reproduction fabrics—or your spare time—go to waste. This 36"-square wall hanging lets you put all your leftovers to good use in one quilt. Be sure to incorporate the full palette of Civil War–era colors: red, blue, burgundy, black, sour or poison green, gold, rust, pink, double pink, and brown—plus all of those shirting prints!

Continued on page 19

Continued from page 17

Cutting for 1 Reverse Nine Patch Block
Cut 53 blocks total.

From *1* of the light prints, cut:
5 squares, 1¼" x 1¼"

From *1* of the dark prints, cut:
4 squares, 1¼" x 1¼"

Cutting for Flag Block
From *1* of the blue prints, cut:
1 rectangle, 1¾" x 2¾"

From *1* of the red prints, cut:
3 rectangles, ¾" x 2¾"
2 rectangles, ¾" x 5"

From *1* of the light prints, cut:
2 rectangles, ¾" x 2¾"
2 rectangles, ¾" x 5"

Cutting for Nine Patch Rows
From *1* of the red prints, cut:
4 squares, 2¾" x 2¾"

Cutting for Binding
From the dark-brown print, cut:
4 strips, 2¼" x 42"

Making the Star Blocks
Use one light (or medium-light) and one dark (or medium) print for each block.

1. Draw a diagonal line on the wrong side of each dark 1¼" square. Place a marked square on a light rectangle, right sides together. Sew on the drawn line. Trim the outside corner of the connector square only, ¼" from the stitched line. Press the seam allowances toward the corner. Repeat on the other end of the rectangle. Make four units.

Make 4.

2. Lay out the units from step 1, four light 1¼" squares, and one dark 2" square in rows. Join the pieces into rows and press the seam allowances as indicated. Join the rows and press. The block should measure 3½" x 3½". Make 45 blocks.

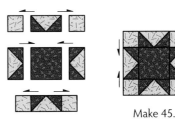

Make 45.

Making the Nine-Patch Star Blocks
Randomly select five Star blocks and four dark 3½" spacer squares and arrange them in a nine-patch arrangement, starting with a Star block in the top-left corner and alternating the blocks with the dark squares. Sew the blocks and plain squares together into rows, pressing the seam allowances toward the dark squares. Sew the rows together to complete a Nine-Patch Star block. Press the seam allowances toward the center. The block should measure 9½" x 9½". Make nine blocks.

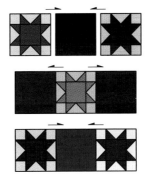 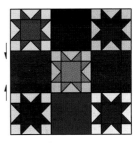

Make 9.

Making the Nine Patch Blocks
1. Sew five matching dark 1¼" squares and four matching light 1¼" squares together into rows. Press the seam allowances toward the darker fabrics. Sew the rows together to make a Nine Patch block. Press the seam allowances in one direction. Make 53 blocks.

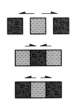

Make 53.

2. Sew five matching light 1¼" squares and four matching dark 1¼" squares together into rows. Press the seam allowances toward the darker fabrics. Sew the rows together to make a reverse Nine Patch block. Press the seam allowances in one direction. Make 53 blocks.

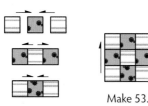

Make 53.

Making the Nine Patch Sashing

Randomly select two Nine Patch blocks and two reverse Nine Patch blocks. Sew the blocks together, alternating them as shown to make a sashing strip. Press the seam allowances in one direction. The sashing strip should measure 2¾" x 9½". Make 12 strips.

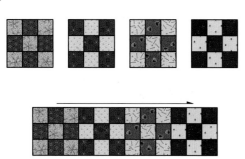

Make 12.

Making the Flag Block

1. Sew the three red and two light ¾" x 2¾" rectangles together along their long edges. Press the seam allowances toward the red rectangles.

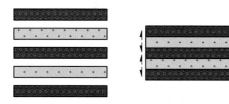

2. Sew the two red and two light ¾" x 5" rectangles together along their long edges. Press the seam allowances toward the red rectangles.

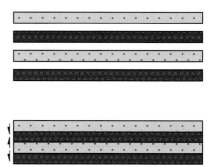

3. Sew the blue 1¾" x 2¾" rectangle to the left side of the unit from step 1. Press the seam allowances toward the blue rectangle. Sew this unit to the top edge of the unit from step 2 to complete the Flag block.

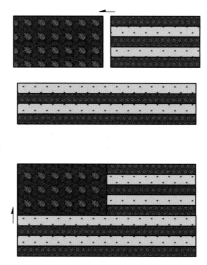

Make 1.

Assembling and Finishing the Quilt

1. Randomly select seven Nine Patch blocks and seven reverse Nine Patch blocks and sew them together, starting with a reverse Nine Patch block and alternating the blocks to make a side border. Press the seam allowances in one direction. Repeat to make a second side border. In the same way, join eight Nine Patch blocks and eight reverse Nine Patch blocks to make the bottom border.

2. Sew the Flag block, seven Nine Patch blocks, and seven reverse Nine Patch blocks together to make the top border of the quilt. Press the seam allowances in one direction.

Side borders
Make 2.

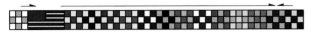

Top border

Bottom border

3. Arrange the blocks and sashing strips on a design wall or the floor. Position the red 2¾" squares between the sashing strips as shown in the quilt-assembly diagram below.

4. Once you're satisfied with the color placement, sew the blocks and sashing strips together into rows. Press the seam allowances toward the sashing strips. Join the rows. Press the seam allowances toward the sashing rows.

5. Sew the side borders to the quilt top first, and then add the top and bottom borders. Press the seam allowances toward the borders.

6. Layer the backing, batting, and quilt top. Baste, and then quilt as desired.

7. Using the dark-brown 2¼"-wide strips, make and attach binding.

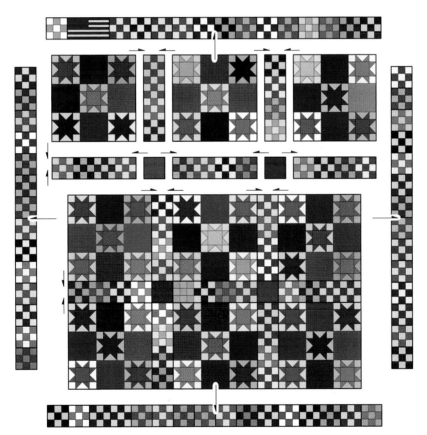

Quilt assembly

Gather the Troops

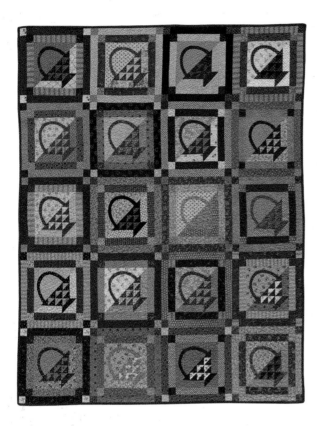

Recruit your bits of reproduction fabrics to make this quilt featuring 20 gathering baskets. Fat eighths will provide faithful service in this handsome wall hanging or lap-sized quilt.

Quilt size: 40½" x 50½"
Finished blocks: 10" x 10"

Materials

Yardage is based on 42"-wide fabric. Fat eighths are approximately 9" x 21".
1 fat eighth *each* of 22 assorted light prints for blocks
1 fat eighth *each* of 20 assorted dark prints for blocks
1 fat eighth *each* of 8 assorted medium prints
    for blocks

⅜ yard of brown print for binding
2⅝ yards of fabric for backing (pieced horizontally)
44" x 54" piece of batting
Template plastic
Freezer paper or fusible web (optional)

Cutting

Measurements include ¼"-wide seam allowances. Make a template of the basket handle pattern (page 25) and prepare the handle for hand or fusible appliqué.

From *each of 10* light prints, cut:
1 square, 6⅞" x 6⅞" (10 total); cut the square in half
    diagonally to yield 2 triangles (20 total)
4 rectangles, 1½" x 6½" (40 total)
8 squares, 1½" x 1½" (80 total)

From *each of 10* medium or light prints, cut:
4 rectangles, 1½" x 8½" (40 total)
4 squares, 1⅞" x 1⅞" (40 total); cut the squares in
    half diagonally to yield 8 triangles (80 total)
1 square, 2⅞" x 2⅞" (10 total); cut the square in half
    diagonally to yield 2 triangles (20 total; 10 will be
    left over)
2 rectangles, 1½" x 3½" (20 total)

From *each of the 10* remaining medium or light prints, cut:
4 squares, 1⅞" x 1⅞" (40 total); cut the squares in
    half diagonally to yield 8 triangles (80 total)
1 square, 2⅞" x 2⅞" (10 total); cut the square in half
    diagonally to yield 2 triangles (20 total; 10 will be
    left over)
2 rectangles, 1½" x 3½" (20 total)

From the assorted dark prints, cut:
20 sets of 6 matching squares, 1⅞" x 1⅞" (120 total);
    cut the squares in half diagonally to yield 12
    matching triangles (240 total)
10 sets of 4 matching rectangles, 1½" x 8½" (40 total)
10 sets of 4 matching rectangles, 1½" x 6½" (40 total)
20 sets of 4 matching squares, 1½" x 1½" (80 total)
20 basket handles

From the brown print, cut:
5 strips, 2¼" x 42"

Making the Basket Bases

Use one dark and two light (or medium) prints for each unit.

1. Sew a light (or medium) 1⅞" triangle to a dark triangle to make a half-square-triangle unit. Press the seam allowances toward the dark triangle. Make six matching units.

Make 6.

2. Lay out the half-square-triangle units and four dark triangles in four rows as shown. Join the triangles and units into rows. Join the rows, adding a dark triangle to the top of the basket. Press the seam allowances as indicated.

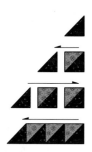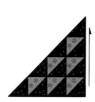

Make 1.

3. Using two light 1½" x 3½" rectangles and two matching light 1⅞" triangles, join a light triangle, a dark triangle, and a light rectangle to make a side unit. Repeat to make a reversed side unit.

Make 1 of each.

4. Join the side units from step 3 to the basket from step 2 as shown. Using a light 2⅞" triangle that matches the side units, sew the triangle to the base of the basket. Press the seam allowances as indicated. Make 20.

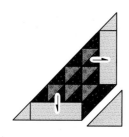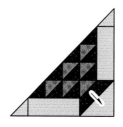

Make 20.

Completing the Basket Blocks

For more information on appliqué techniques, visit ShopMartingale.com/HowtoQuilt for free downloadable instructions.

1. Using your favorite appliqué method, appliqué a dark basket handle to a light 6⅞" triangle. Make 20.

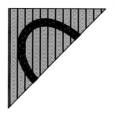

Make 20.

2. Join an appliquéd triangle from step 1 to a basket base to make a basket unit. Press the seam allowances toward the handle. Make 20.

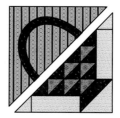

Make 20.

3. Select four matching light 1½" x 6½" rectangles and four matching dark 1½" squares. Sew rectangles to the left and right sides of a basket unit. Press the seam allowances toward the rectangles. Sew a dark square to each end of the two remaining rectangles. Press the seam allowances toward the rectangles. Sew these units to the top and bottom of the basket unit. Press the seam allowances toward the rectangles. Make 10.

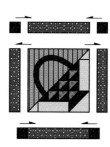

Make 10.

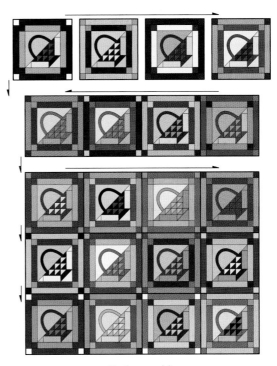

4. Select four matching dark 1½" x 8½" rectangles and four matching light 1½" squares. Sew rectangles to the left and right sides of a basket unit from step 3. Press the seam allowances toward the rectangles. Sew a light square to each end of the two remaining rectangles. Press the seam allowances toward the rectangles. Sew these units to the top and bottom of the basket unit. Press the seam allowances toward the rectangles. Make 10 blocks.

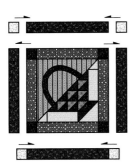

Make 10.

5. Repeat steps 3 and 4, using four matching dark 1½" x 6½" rectangles, four matching light 1½" squares, four matching light 1½" x 8½" rectangles, and four matching dark 1½" squares to make 10 blocks as shown.

Quilt assembly

Make 10.

Assembling and Finishing the Quilt

1. Arrange the blocks in five rows of four blocks each, alternating light and dark as shown in the quilt-assembly diagram above right.

2. Sew the blocks together into rows, pressing the seam allowances in opposite directions from row to row. Join the rows. Press the seam allowances in one direction.

3. Layer the backing, batting, and quilt top. Baste, and then quilt as desired.

4. Using the brown 2¼"-wide strips, make and attach binding.

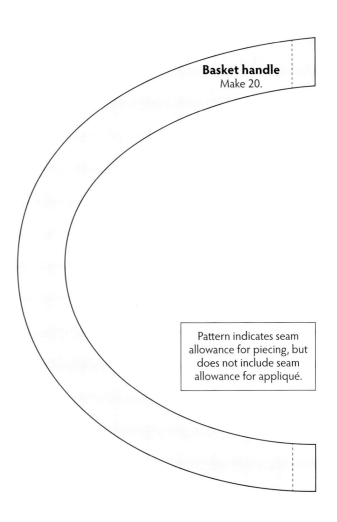

Basket handle
Make 20.

Pattern indicates seam allowance for piecing, but does not include seam allowance for appliqué.

Devil's Claw

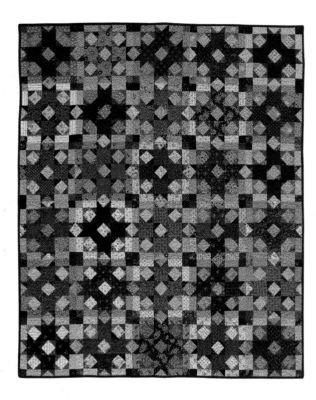

Quilt size: 40½" x 48½"

Finished blocks: 8" x 8"

Materials

Yardage is based on 42"-wide fabric. Fat quarters are approximately 18" x 21".

1 fat quarter *each* of 15 assorted dark prints in red, navy, gold, orange, and light blue for blocks

1 fat quarter *each* of 15 assorted light or medium-light prints for blocks

⅜ yard of navy print for binding

2½ yards of fabric for backing (pieced horizontally)

44" x 52" piece of batting

Cutting

Measurements include ¼"-wide seam allowances.

From the assorted dark prints, cut:

30 sets of 4 matching squares, 2½" x 2½" (120 total)

960 squares, 1½" x 1½"

From the assorted light or medium-light prints, cut:

30 sets of 5 matching squares, 2½" x 2½" (150 total)

30 sets of 4 matching rectangles, 1½" x 2½" (120 total)

30 sets of 8 matching rectangles, 1½" x 2½" (240 total)

From the navy print, cut:

5 strips, 2¼" x 42"

Making the Devil's Claw Blocks

1. Select four matching light 1½" x 2½" rectangles and eight dark 1½" squares. Draw a diagonal line on the wrong side of each dark square. Place a marked square on a light rectangle, right sides together. Sew on the drawn line. Trim the outside corner of the square only, ¼" from the stitched

The Devil's Claw quilt block has been around since the mid-1800s, making it a perfect choice to stitch using Civil War reproduction fabrics. The name Devil's Claw is based on a plant from South Africa, so quilters during the Civil War era may have had another term for the block, such as Botch Handle. That name refers to the handles used to lift lids off of old woodstoves and seems much more apropos to the period. Either way, this version is truly a scrap lover's dream!

line. Press the seam allowances toward the corner. Repeat on the other end of the rectangle. Make four units.

Make 4.

2. Select five matching light 2½" squares and 20 assorted dark 1½" squares. Sew four dark squares to each light square using the method described in step 1 to make five square-in-a-square units. Press the seam allowances toward the corners. Make five units.

Make 5.

3. Select four matching 2½" dark squares, eight matching light 1½" x 2½" rectangles, and four dark 1½" squares. Join the squares, rectangles, and units from steps 1 and 2 into rows. Sew the rows together. Press the seam allowances as indicated. Make 30 blocks.

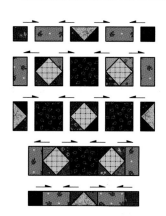 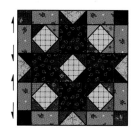

Make 30.

Assembling and Finishing the Quilt

1. Arrange the Devil's Claw blocks in six rows of five blocks each.

2. Sew the blocks together into rows, pressing the seam allowances in opposite directions from row to row. Join the rows. Press the seam allowances in one direction.

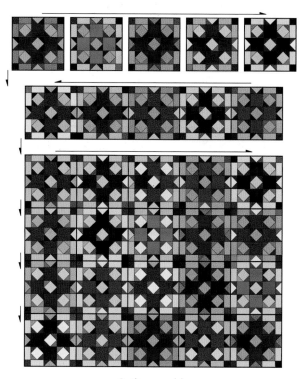

Quilt assembly

3. Layer the backing, batting, and quilt top. Baste, and then quilt as desired.

4. Using the navy 2¼"-wide strips, make and attach binding.

Lady of the Lake

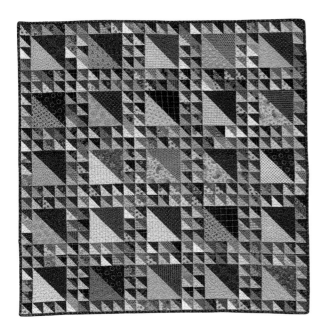

Quilt size: 38" x 38"
Finished blocks: 7½" x 7½"

Materials
Yardage is based on 42"-wide fabric.
¼ yard *each* of 10 assorted light prints for blocks
¼ yard *each* of 10 assorted dark prints in red, orange, pink, gold, blue, navy, black, and gray for blocks
⅜ yard of dark-blue print for binding
1¼ yards of fabric for backing
42" x 42" piece of batting

Cutting
Measurements include ¼"-wide seam allowances.

From the assorted light prints, cut:
13 squares, 5⅜" x 5⅜"; cut the squares in half diagonally to yield 26 triangles (1 will be left over)
200 squares, 2⅜" x 2⅜"; cut the squares in half diagonally to yield 400 triangles

From the assorted dark prints, cut:
13 squares, 5⅜" x 5⅜"; cut the squares in half diagonally to yield 26 triangles (1 will be left over)
200 squares, 2⅜" x 2⅜"; cut the squares in half diagonally to yield 400 triangles

From the dark-blue print, cut:
5 strips, 2¼" x 42"

Making the Lady of the Lake Blocks
1. Sew a light 2⅜" triangle to a dark 2⅜" triangle. Press the seam allowances toward the dark triangle. Make 16.

Make 16.

Named for Sir Walter Scott's poem *Lady of the Lake,* which drew on the legend of King Arthur and was published in 1810, this quilt block became popular in the 19th century. It's easy to see why: it's a perfect way for thrifty seamstresses and quiltmakers to use up their scraps! If your scrap bin is overflowing, put those tidbits to good use. Or, start fresh with a collection of Civil War reproduction fat quarters to make this little showstopper.

2. Sew a light 5⅜" triangle to a dark 5⅜" triangle. Press the seam allowances toward the dark triangle.

3. Join the units from steps 1 and 2, making sure to orient them as shown. Press the seam allowances as indicated. Make 25 blocks.

Make 2 of each.

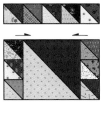

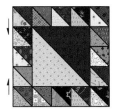

Make 25.

Assembling and Finishing the Quilt

1. Arrange the blocks in five rows of five blocks each. Sew the blocks together into rows, pressing the seam allowances in opposite directions from row to row. Join the rows. Press the seam allowances in one direction.

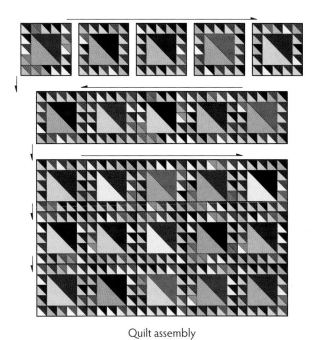

Quilt assembly

2. Layer the backing, batting, and quilt top. Baste, and then quilt as desired.

3. Using the dark-blue 2¼"-wide strips, make and attach binding.

Crossroads

This dandy little quilt—just 30" square—is stitched in shades of gray, blue, and red to help celebrate not only our country's independence, but also the fact that the United States emerged from the Civil War united, even after the nation's greatest period of strife. Make this as a wall hanging or table topper to commemorate your favorite patriot or patriotic holiday.

Quilt size: 30½" x 30½"
Finished blocks: 11½" x 11½"

Materials

Yardage is based on 42"-wide fabric. Fat quarters are approximately 18" x 21".
1 fat quarter *each* of 13 assorted dark prints in blue, gray, and red for blocks, cornerstones, and pieced border
1 fat quarter *each* of 6 assorted light and medium-light prints for blocks and pieced outer border
⅓ yard of red stripe for inner border
⅓ yard of dark-blue print for binding
1 yard of fabric for backing
34" x 34" piece of batting

Cutting

Measurements include ¼"-wide seam allowances.

Cutting for 1 Nine Patch Block

Cut 16 blocks total.

From *1* of the dark prints, cut:
4 squares, 1¾" x 1¾"

From *1* of the light or medium-light prints, cut:
5 squares, 1¾" x 1¾"

Cutting for 1 Center Cross Block

Cut 4 blocks total.

From *1* of the light or medium-light prints, cut:
1 square, 3⅝" x 3⅝"; cut the square into quarters diagonally to yield 4 triangles

From *1* of the dark prints, cut:
4 rectangles, 1¾" x 3"

From *1* of the dark prints, cut:
1 square, 1¾" x 1¾"

Cutting for Rail Fence Blocks

Cut 16 blocks total.

From the assorted dark, light, and medium-light prints, cut:
48 rectangles, 1¾" x 4½"

Cutting for Inner Border

From the red stripe, cut:
4 strips, 2" x 23½"

From the dark prints, cut:
4 squares, 2" x 2"

Cutting for Outer Border

From the dark prints, cut:
26 squares, 2⅞" x 2⅞"; cut the squares in half diagonally to yield 52 triangles
4 matching squares, 2½" x 2½"

From the light and medium-light prints, cut:
26 squares, 2⅞" x 2⅞"; cut the squares in half diagonally to yield 52 triangles

Cutting for Binding

From the dark-blue print, cut:
4 strips, 2¼" x 42"

Making the Nine-Patch Units

Use five light 1¾" squares and four matching dark 1¾" squares for each unit.

Sew the squares together in rows, pressing the seam allowances toward the darker fabrics. Sew the rows together to make a nine-patch unit. Press the seam allowances toward the center. The unit should measure 4¼" x 4¼". Make 16.

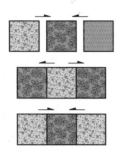

Make 16.

Making the Center Cross Units

1. Using four matching light (or medium-light) 3⅝" triangles and four matching dark 1¾" x 3" rectangles, sew the light triangles, dark rectangles, and a dark 1¾" square together to make a center cross unit. Press the seam allowances as indicated.

2. Trim and square up the unit to measure 4½" x 4½". Make four.

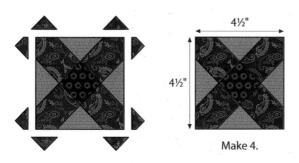

Make 4.

Making the Rail Fence Units

Randomly sew three dark, light, and/or medium-light 1¾" x 4½" rectangles together along their long edges. Press the seam allowances as indicated. The block should measure 4½" x 4¼". Make 16.

Make 16.

Making the Crossroad Blocks

Randomly select four nine-patch units, four rail fence units, and one center cross unit, and lay them out in a nine-patch arrangement as shown. Sew the units together into rows, pressing the seam allowances toward the rail fence units. Sew the rows together to complete a Crossroad block. Press the seam allowances away from the center. The block should measure 12" x 12". Make four blocks.

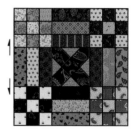

Make 4.

Assembling and Finishing the Quilt

1. Sew a pair of light and dark 2⅞" triangles together. Press the seam allowances toward the dark triangle. Make 52 half-square-triangle units.

2. Sew 13 half-square-triangle units together, orienting the dark triangles in the same direction. Press the seam allowances in one direction. Make four pieced borders.

Make 4.

3. Arrange the Crossroads blocks in two rows of two blocks each. Sew the blocks together into rows, pressing the seam allowances in opposite directions from row to row. Join the rows and press the seam allowances in one direction as shown in the quilt-assembly diagram below.

4. Sew the red-striped 2"-wide strips to the top and bottom of the quilt top. Press the seam allowances toward the border strips. Sew a dark 2" square to each end of the two remaining striped strips. Press the seam allowances toward the strips. Sew these strips to the sides of the quilt top. Press the seam allowances toward the border strips.

5. Sew pieced border strips from step 2 to the top and bottom of the quilt top with the light edge of each strip toward the inner border. Press the seam allowances toward the inner border. Sew a dark 2½" square to each end of the two remaining pieced strips. Press the seam allowances toward the dark squares. Sew these strips to the sides of the quilt top. Press the seam allowances toward the inner border.

6. Layer the backing, batting, and quilt top. Baste, and then quilt as desired.

7. Using the dark-blue 2¼"-wide strips, make and attach binding.

Quilt assembly

Dixie

Celebrate the heart of Dixie with a complex-looking quilt that's made with just three simple units—four patches, hourglass units, and triangle squares. Whether you have a collection of reproduction fabrics waiting to be used or lots of scraps left over from other projects, this quilt is fun to put together bit by bit.

Quilt size: 40½" x 40½"
Finished blocks: 4" x 4"

Materials
Yardage is based on 42"-wide fabric.
⅛ yard *each* of 24 assorted dark prints in navy, blue, light blue, teal, brown, red, maroon, red-orange, and black for blocks and pieced border
⅛ yard *each* of 24 assorted light prints in white, cream, tan, gold, medium-red, blue, and brown for blocks and pieced border
⅜ yard of tan print for binding
2⅝ yards of fabric for backing
44" x 44" piece of batting

Cutting
Measurements include ¼"-wide seam allowances.

From the dark prints, cut:
82 squares, 3¼" x 3¼"; cut the squares into quarters diagonally to yield 328 triangles
40 sets of 2 matching squares, 2½" x 2½" (80 total)
38 squares, 2⅞" x 2⅞"; cut the squares in half diagonally to yield 76 triangles

From the light prints, cut:
82 squares, 3¼" x 3¼"; cut the squares into quarters diagonally to yield 328 triangles
40 sets of 2 matching squares, 2½" x 2½" (80 total)
38 squares, 2⅞" x 2⅞"; cut the squares in half diagonally to yield 76 triangles

From the tan print, cut:
5 strips, 2¼" x 42"

Making the Hourglass Blocks

Use one light and one dark print for each unit.

1. Join two light triangles and two dark triangles to make an hourglass unit. Press the seam allowances as indicated. The unit should measure 2½" x 2½". Make 164 units.

Make 164.

> ## MIX IT UP
>
> *You can use the same prints in a unit or, for a more antique look, mix up some of the fabrics as we did. You can also sew a few Hourglass blocks together incorrectly.*

2. Randomly select four hourglass units and lay them out in a four-patch arrangement, rotating the units so that the light and dark triangles alternate positions. Sew the units together into rows. Press the seam allowances toward the darker triangles. Sew the rows together and press the seam allowances in one direction. Make 41 blocks.

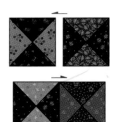 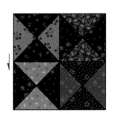

Make 41.

Making the Four Patch Blocks

Using two matching light 2½" squares and two matching dark 2½" squares, sew the squares together to make a Four Patch block as shown. Press the seam allowances as indicated. Make 40 blocks.

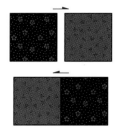 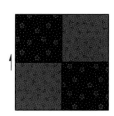

Make 40.

Assembling and Finishing the Quilt

1. Sew a pair of light and dark 2⅞" triangles together. Press the seam allowances toward the dark triangle. Make 76 half-square-triangle units.

Make 76.

2. Sew 18 half-square-triangle units together, orienting the dark triangles in the same direction to make the top border. Sew 18 units together, reversing the direction of the dark triangles to make the bottom border. Sew 20 half-square-triangle units together in the same manner to make a side border. Make two side borders. Press all seam allowances in one direction.

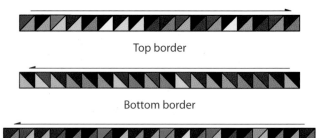

Top border

Bottom border

Side borders
Make 2.

3. Alternating Hourglass and Four Patch blocks, arrange the blocks in nine rows of nine blocks each. Rearrange the blocks until you are pleased with the color placement. Sew the blocks together into rows, pressing the seam allowances toward the Four Patch blocks. Join the rows and press the seam allowances in one direction.

4. Sew the top, bottom, and side border strips to the quilt top, orienting the strips as shown in the quilt-assembly diagram below. Press the seam allowances toward the quilt top.

5. Layer the backing, batting, and quilt top. Baste, and then quilt as desired.

6. Using the tan 2¼"-wide strips, make and attach binding.

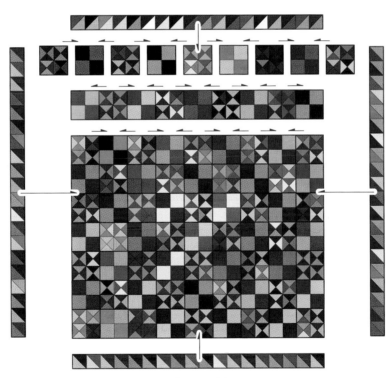

Quilt assembly

Line Up

Materials

Yardage is based on 42"-wide fabric.

2¾ yards *total* of assorted light prints for blocks and pieced middle border

2¾ yards *total* of assorted dark prints for blocks and pieced middle border

1⅛ yards of tan print for inner and outer borders

½ yard of dark-red print for binding

3¼ yards of fabric for backing (pieced horizontally)

54" x 70" piece of batting

Cutting

Measurements include ¼"-wide seam allowances.

From the assorted light prints, cut:

59 sets of 2 matching squares, 2⅞" x 2⅞" (118 total); cut the squares in half diagonally to yield 4 matching triangles (236 total)

29 squares, 4⅞" x 4⅞"; cut the squares in half diagonally to yield 58 triangles

46 squares, 2⅞" x 2⅞"; cut the squares in half diagonally to yield 92 triangles

From the assorted dark prints, cut:

59 sets of 2 matching squares, 2⅞" x 2⅞" (118 total); cut the squares in half diagonally to yield 4 matching triangles (236 total)

29 squares, 4⅞" x 4⅞"; cut the squares in half diagonally to yield 58 triangles

46 squares, 2⅞" x 2⅞"; cut the squares in half diagonally to yield 92 triangles

4 squares, 2½" x 2½"

From the tan print, cut:

2 strips, 1½" x 36½"

3 strips, 1½" x 42"

6 strips, 4½" x 42"

From the dark-red print, cut:

2¼"-wide bias strips, enough to yield 245" of binding

Lining up in formation is one of the first instructions a soldier learns. In this quilt, that instruction is taken to heart, as pinwheels and triangles are aligned in neat diagonal rows. You can plan the color scheme to give your quilt a more regimented appearance, or take our cue and make this entirely from your scrap basket.

Quilt size: 50½" x 66½"

Finished blocks: 4" x 4"

Making the Pinwheel Blocks

Use four matching light 2⅞" triangles and four matching dark 2⅞" triangles for each block.

1. Join one light and one dark triangle. Press the seam allowances toward the dark triangle. Make four half-square-triangle units.

Make 4.

2. Sew the triangle units together as shown to make a Pinwheel block. Press the seam allowances as indicated. The block should measure 4½" x 4½". Make 59 blocks.

Make 59.

Making the Triangle Blocks

Sew a pair of light and dark 4⅞" triangles together. Press the seam allowances toward the dark triangle. Make 58 Triangle blocks.

Make 58.

Assembling and Finishing the Quilt

1. Sew a pair of light and dark 2⅞" triangles together. Press the seam allowances toward the dark triangle. Make 92 half-square-triangle units.

2. Sew 19 half-square-triangle units together, orienting the dark triangles in the same direction. Make two borders for the top and bottom of the quilt. Sew 27 half-square-triangle units together in the same manner, and sew a dark 2½" square to each end. Make two side borders.

Make 2.

Make 2.

3. Arrange the Pinwheel and Triangle blocks in 13 rows of nine blocks each, alternating the blocks as shown in the quilt-assembly diagram on page 43. Rearrange the blocks until you are pleased with the color placement. Sew the blocks together into rows, pressing the seam allowances in opposite directions from row to row. Join the rows and press the seam allowances in one direction. The quilt top should measure 36½" x 52½".

4. Sew the tan 1½" x 36½" strips to the top and bottom of the quilt. Press the seam allowances toward the tan strips. Join the three tan 1½" x 42" strips end to end. From the pieced strips, cut two 54½"-long strips and sew them to the left and right sides of the quilt. Press the seam allowances toward the tan strips.

5. Sew the 19-unit border strips to the top and bottom of the quilt top with the dark edge of each strip toward the inner border. Press the seam allowances toward the inner border. Sew the 27-unit strips to the sides of the quilt in the same manner. The quilt top should measure 42½" x 58½".

6. Join the tan 4½"-wide strips end to end. From the pieced strip, cut two 42½"-long strips and two 66½"-long strips. Sew the strips to the top, bottom, and sides of the quilt top. Press the seam allowances toward the outer border.

7. Layer the backing, batting, and quilt top. Baste, and then quilt as desired.

8. You can leave the quilt top square, or round the corners as we did. Place a 5"-diameter plate or cardboard circle on the corner and trace the curve. Trim the corner on the drawn line.

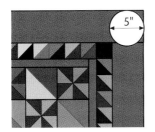

9. Using the dark-red 2¼"-wide strips, make and attach binding.

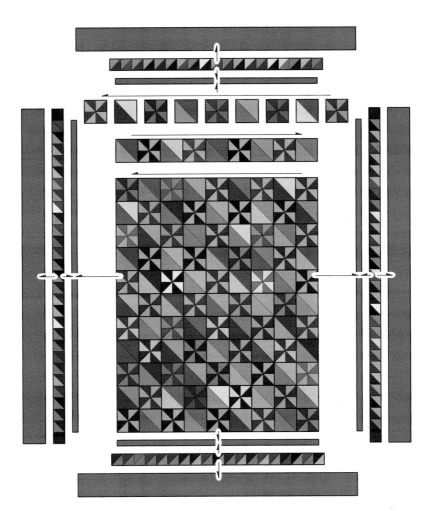

Quilt assembly

Opposition

Quilt size: 30½" x 30½"
Finished blocks: 6" x 6"

Materials

Yardage is based on 42"-wide fabric.
⅛ yard *each* of 39 assorted light, medium, and dark prints for blocks and pieced border
⅝ yard of green print for setting triangles and inner border
⅓ yard of blue print for binding
1 yard of fabric for backing
34" x 34" piece of batting

Cutting

Measurements include ¼"-wide seam allowances.

Cutting for 1 Star Block

Cut 13 blocks total.

From *1* of the assorted prints, cut:
1 square, 2½" x 2½"
8 squares, 1½" x 1½"

From *1* of the assorted prints, cut:
4 rectangles, 1½" x 2½"
4 squares, 1½" x 1½"

From *1* of the dark prints, cut:
8 squares, 1⅞" x 1⅞"; cut the squares in half diagonally to yield 16 triangles
2 squares, 1½" x 1½"

From *1* of the light prints, cut:
8 squares, 1⅞" x 1⅞"; cut the squares in half diagonally to yield 16 triangles
2 squares, 1½" x 1½"

Continued on page 46

Sawtooth Stars surrounded by tiny triangle squares symbolize troops rallying around their land, their homes, and their base, providing protection against the opposition. We can't imagine any quilter opposing this quilt set on a background of our favorite sour green. But if that green's too much for you, change the background color to one that you love!

Continued from page 44

Cutting for Setting Triangles and Inner Border

From the green print, cut:

2 squares, 10¾" x 10¾"; cut the squares into quarters
diagonally to yield 8 side triangles*

2 squares, 6½" x 6½"; cut the squares in half
diagonally to yield 4 corner triangles*

2 strips, 1¼" x 26"

2 strips, 1¼" x 27½"

*The side and corner triangles are slightly oversized and
will be trimmed later.*

Cutting for Pieced Border and Binding

From the assorted dark prints, cut:

36 squares, 2⅜" x 2⅜"; cut the squares in half
diagonally to yield 72 triangles

From the assorted light prints, cut:

36 squares, 2⅜" x 2⅜"; cut the squares in half
diagonally to yield 72 triangles

From the assorted medium prints, cut:

4 squares, 2" x 2"

From the blue print, cut:

4 strips, 2¼" x 42"

Making the Star Blocks

For each center star unit, select one print for the star
and a contrasting print for the background.

1. Draw a diagonal line on the wrong side of eight
   star 1½" squares. Place a marked square on a
   background 1½" x 2½" rectangle, right sides
   together. Sew on the drawn line. Trim the outside
   corner of the square only, ¼" from the stitched
   line. Press the seam allowances toward the corner.
   Repeat on the other end of the rectangle. Make
   four units.

Make 4.

2. Join the four units from step 1, four background
   1½" squares, and one star 2½" square in rows.
   Press the seam allowances as indicated. The block
   should measure 4½" x 4½".

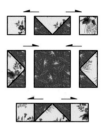

3. Sew 16 matching light 1⅞" triangles to 16
   matching dark 1⅞" triangles to make 16 half-
   square-triangle units. Press the seam allowances
   toward the dark triangles.

Make 16.

4. Join the center star unit, the half-square-triangle
   units, two light 1½" squares that match the
   triangle units, and two dark 1½" squares that
   match the triangle units. Press the seam
   allowances as indicated. Make 13 blocks.

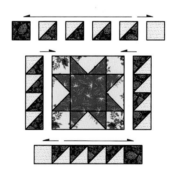 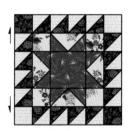

Make 13.

Assembling and Finishing the Quilt

1. Sew a pair of light and dark 2⅜" triangles together. Press the seam allowances toward the dark triangle. Make 72 units.

2. Sew 18 half-square-triangle units together, orienting the dark triangles in the same direction. Make four border strips.

Make 4.

3. Sew a medium 2" square to each end of a border strip from step 2 to make a side border strip. Press the seam allowances toward the squares. Make two side borders.

Make 2.

4. Arrange the blocks and the green side and corner triangles in diagonal rows as shown. Sew the blocks and side triangles into rows. Join the rows and add the corner triangles last. Press the seam allowances as indicated. Trim the oversized triangles all around, leaving an equal amount from the block corners so that the quilt top measures 26" x 26". You'll need this size for the pieced triangle border to fit properly.

Quilt assembly

5. Sew the green 1¼" x 26" strips to the top and bottom of the quilt top. Press the seam allowances toward the border strips. Sew the green 1¼" x 27½" strips to the quilt sides in the same manner.

6. Sew the 18-unit border strips from step 2 to the top and bottom of the quilt top. Press the seam allowances toward the inner border. Sew the border strips from step 3 to the quilt sides in the same manner.

Quilt plan

7. Layer the backing, batting, and quilt top. Baste, and then quilt as desired.

8. Using the blue 2¼"-wide strips, make and attach binding.

Scorched!

These two little projects faithfully represent the doll quilts from long ago that young girls might have played with and cherished during Civil War times. To make these Broken Dishes and Double Four Patch designs look as if they were just pulled out of an antique trunk, we stained the finished quilts in a coffee bath and then literally scorched them with a candle flame in random spots.

Broken Dishes

Quilt size: 16½" x 16½"

Finished blocks: 4" x 4"

Materials

Yardage is based on 42"-wide fabric.

⅓ yard *total* of assorted dark scraps for blocks

⅓ yard *total* of assorted light and medium-light scraps for blocks

¼ yard of pink print for bias binding

⅝ yard of fabric for backing

20" x 20" piece of batting

Cutting

Measurements include ¼"-wide seam allowances.

From the assorted dark scraps, cut:

16 sets of 2 matching squares, 2⅞" x 2⅞" (32 total); cut the squares in half diagonally to yield 4 matching triangles (64 total)

From the assorted light and medium-light scraps, cut:

16 sets of 2 matching squares, 2⅞" x 2⅞" (32 total); cut the squares in half diagonally to yield 4 matching triangles (64 total)

From the pink print, cut:

2¼"-wide bias strips, enough to yield 75" of binding

Making the Broken Dishes Blocks

1. Sew a pair of light and dark 2⅞" triangles together. Press the seam allowances toward the dark triangle. Make 32 sets of two matching half-square-triangle units (64 total).

Make 64.

2. Lay out four units in a four-patch arrangement as shown. You can use four matching units, choose two pairs of matching units, or mix up the units in some blocks as we did. Sew the units together as shown to make a Broken Dishes block. Press the seam allowances as indicated. Make 16 blocks.

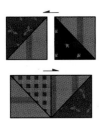 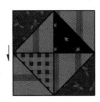

Make 16.

Assembling and Finishing the Quilt

1. Lay out the blocks in four rows of four blocks each, rearranging the blocks until you are pleased with the color placement. Sew the blocks together into rows, pressing the seam allowances in opposite directions from row to row. Join the rows and press the seam allowances in one direction.

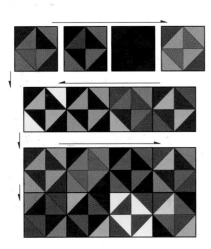

Quilt assembly

2. Layer the backing, batting, and quilt top. Baste, and then quilt as desired.

3. You can leave the quilt square, or round the corners as we did. Place a 5"-diameter plate or cardboard circle on the corner block and trace the curve. Trim the corner on the drawn line.

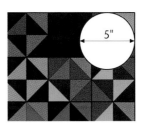

4. Using the pink 2¼"-wide bias-binding strips, make and attach binding.

5. Stain the quilt with a coffee bath and then use a candle flame to *carefully* scorch the quilt in random places.

Four Patch

Quilt size: 14½" x 16½"

Finished blocks: 2" x 2"

Materials

Yardage is based on 42"-wide fabric.

¼ yard *total* of assorted dark scraps for blocks

¼ yard *total* of assorted light and medium-light scraps for blocks and spacer squares

¼ yard of brown print for border

¼ yard of navy print for binding

⅝ yard of fabric for backing

18" x 20" piece of batting

Cutting

Measurements include ¼"-wide seam allowances.

From the assorted light and medium-light scraps, cut:

15 squares, 2½" x 2½"

30 squares, 1½" x 1½"

From the assorted dark scraps, cut:

30 squares, 1½" x 1½"

From the brown print, cut:

2 strips, 2½" x 10½"

2 strips, 2½" x 16½"

From the navy print, cut:

2 strips, 2¼" x 42"

Making the Four Patch Blocks

Select two light and two dark 1½" squares. You can use two pairs of matching squares or mix up the squares in some blocks as we did. Sew the squares together to make a Four Patch block. Press the seam allowances as indicated. Make 15 blocks.

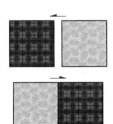 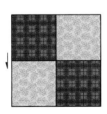

Make 15.

Assembling and Finishing the Quilt

1. Arrange the Four Patch blocks and light 2½" squares in six rows, alternating them as shown in the quilt-assembly diagram below. Sew the blocks and squares together into rows. Press the seam allowances toward the spacer squares. Join the rows and press the seam allowances in one direction.

2. Sew the brown 2½" x 10½" strips to the top and bottom of the quilt top. Press the seam allowances toward the brown strips. Sew the brown 2½" x 16½" strips to the sides of the quilt top. Press the seam allowances toward the border strips.

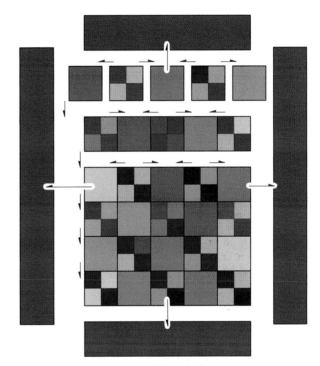

Quilt assembly

3. Layer the backing, batting, and quilt top. Baste, and then quilt as desired.

4. Using the navy 2¼"-wide strips, make and attach binding.

5. Stain the quilt with a coffee bath and then use a candle flame to *carefully* scorch the quilt in random places.

Quest for Freedom

Freedom—it's what the Civil War was fought for, whether you were on the side fighting for the right to own slaves and preserve a way of life, or the side fighting to preserve the Union and liberate every person from the bonds of slavery. Some types of freedom are fundamental, while others are nonessential but certainly nice—such as freedom from stress! That's what you'll enjoy as you sew this simple Nine Patch quilt, with blocks and setting squares that go together easily.

Quilt size: 51½" x 57¾"

Finished blocks: 4½" x 4½"

Materials

Yardage is based on 42"-wide fabric. Fat eighths are approximately 9" x 21".

⅛ yard *each* (or scraps) of 18 assorted dark prints in orange, gold, chrome yellow, red, black, brown, burgundy, spring green, and navy for blocks

1 yard *total* of assorted light and medium-light prints for blocks

1 yard *total* of assorted dark-brown prints for setting triangles and binding

¼ yard *each* of 4 assorted red prints for spacer squares

¼ yard *each* of 3 assorted medium-brown and/or gray prints for spacer squares

¼ yard *each* of 2 assorted navy prints for spacer squares

3¼ yards of fabric for backing (pieced horizontally)

54" x 62" piece of batting

Cutting

Measurements include ¼"-wide seam allowances.

Cutting for 1 Reverse Nine Patch Block

Cut 20 blocks total.

From the assorted light and medium-light prints, cut:
5 squares, 2" x 2"

From the assorted dark prints, cut:
4 squares, 2" x 2"

Cutting for 1 Nine Patch Block

Cut 22 blocks total.

From the assorted dark prints, cut:
5 squares, 2" x 2"

From the assorted light and medium-light prints, cut:
4 squares, 2" x 2"

Continued on page 54

Continued from page 52

Cutting for 1 Four Patch Block

Cut 30 blocks total.

From the assorted dark prints, cut:
2 squares, 2¾" x 2¾"

From the assorted light and medium-light prints, cut:
2 squares, 2¾" x 2¾"

Cutting for Spacer Squares, Setting Triangles, and Binding

From the navy prints, cut:
12 squares, 5" x 5"

From the assorted medium-brown and/or gray prints, cut:
18 squares, 5" x 5"

From the assorted red prints, cut:
26 squares, 5" x 5"

From the dark-brown prints, cut:
8 squares, 8" x 8"; cut the squares into quarters diagonally to yield 32 side triangles (2 will be left over)*
2 squares, 6" x 6"; cut the squares in half diagonally to yield 4 corner triangles*
6 strips, 2¼" x 42"

*The side and corner triangles are slightly oversized and will be trimmed later.

Making the Reverse Nine Patch Blocks

Use five matching light (or medium-light) 2" squares and four matching dark 2" squares for each block.

Sew the squares together into rows, pressing the seam allowances toward the darker fabrics. Sew the rows together to make a reverse Nine Patch block.

Press the seam allowances toward the center. The block should measure 5" x 5". Make 20 blocks.

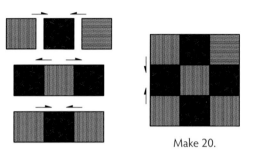

Make 20.

Making the Nine Patch Blocks

Use five matching dark 2" squares and four matching light (or medium-light) 2" squares for each block.

Sew the squares together into rows, pressing the seam allowances toward the darker fabrics. Sew the rows together to make a Nine Patch block. Press the seam allowances away from the center. The block should measure 5" x 5". Make 22 blocks.

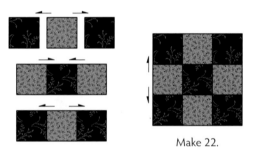

Make 22.

Making the Four Patch Blocks

Use two matching dark 2¾" squares and two matching light (or medium-light) 2¾" squares for each block.

Sew the squares together into rows, pressing the seam allowances toward the darker fabrics. Sew the rows together to make a Four Patch block. Press the seam allowances in one direction. The block should measure 5" x 5". Make 30 blocks.

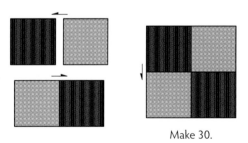

Make 30.

Assembling and Finishing the Quilt

1. Arrange the Nine Patch, reverse Nine Patch, and Four Patch blocks along with the navy, medium-brown (or gray), and red spacer squares in diagonal rows, following the quilt-assembly diagram below for color placement and block orientation. Add the dark-brown side and corner triangles.

2. Sew the blocks, squares, and side triangles into rows. Join the rows and add the corner triangles last. Press the seam allowances as indicated. Trim the oversized triangles all around, leaving ¼" beyond the block corners.

3. Layer the backing, batting, and quilt top. Baste, and then quilt as desired.

4. Using the dark-brown 2¼"-wide strips, make and attach binding.

Quilt assembly

Lessons Learned

Many traditional quilt blocks were named for items or ideals associated with everyday life, and this one is no exception. One-room schoolhouses dotted the landscape in the 1800s and, fortunately, many still stand today. This Schoolhouse block, with three windows and no door, was popular during that time.

Quilt size: 41" x 50½"
Finished blocks: 8" x 8"

Materials

Yardage is based on 42"-wide fabric. Fat quarters are approximately 18" x 21".
1 fat quarter *each* of 20 assorted prints in navy, red, brown, light blue, gray, and cream for blocks and cornerstones
1⅜ yards of blue print for sashing, border, and binding
2¾ yards of fabric for backing (pieced horizontally)
45" x 54" piece of batting
Freezer paper (optional)

Cutting

Measurements include ¼"-wide seam allowances.

Cutting for 1 House Block

Cut 20 blocks total. In each block the house can be dark or light, so the fabrics are listed as "background" and "house." Refer to the photo on page 57 for guidance with fabric placement as needed.

From 1 background fabric, cut:
2 rectangles, 1½" x 2" (chimney row)
1 rectangle, 1½" x 4½" (chimney row)
3 rectangles, 1½" x 2½" (window section)
1 rectangle, 1" x 4½" (window section)
1 rectangle, 1" x 5" (window section)

From 1 house fabric, cut:
2 rectangles, 1" x 1½" (chimney row)
2 rectangles, 1½" x 3½" (window section)
3 rectangles, 1½" x 2½" (window section)
1 rectangle, 1" x 5" (window section)
1 rectangle, 1½" x 5" (window section)
2 rectangles, 1¼" x 2½" (window section)

Cutting for Sashing, Border, and Binding

From 1 cream print, cut:
12 squares, 2" x 2"

From the blue print, cut:
8 strips, 2" x 42"; crosscut into 31 rectangles, 2" x 8½"
2 strips, 2½" x 37"
3 strips, 2½" x 42"
5 strips, 2¼" x 42"

Making the House Blocks

Use one house fabric for each block. You can use one or two background fabrics for each block.

Chimney Row

Sew two background 1½" x 2" rectangles, two house 1" x 1½" rectangles, and one background 1½" x 4½" rectangle together. Press the seam allowances toward the darker fabric. The chimney row should measure 1½" x 8½".

Roof Row

1. Trace the patterns on page 60 onto the paper side of freezer paper. Cut out the templates on the traced line to make one of each shape. Press the freezer-paper templates onto the *right* side of the appropriate fabrics, making sure to leave at least ½" of fabric all around each template. Cut out each shape, adding ¼" for seam allowance on all sides.

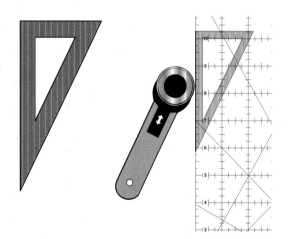

2. With the freezer-paper templates facing each other, match the beginning and ending points on templates A and B. Line up the edges of the templates and pin at each point. Using an accurate ¼" seam allowance, sew the pieces together. Add pieces C–E in the same way. Do not remove the paper templates until the row is complete. Press the seam allowances as indicated and remove the paper templates. The roof row should measure 3½" x 8½".

Window Section

1. Sew two house 1½" x 2½" rectangles and one background 1½" x 2½" rectangle together. Sew house 1½" x 3½" rectangles to the top and bottom of the unit. Then sew a background 1" x 4½" rectangle to the right edge of the unit. Press the seam allowances as indicated. The left window unit should measure 4" x 4½".

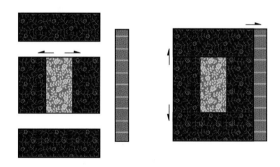

2. Sew two house 1¼" x 2½" rectangles, two background 1½" x 2½" rectangles, and one house 1½" x 2½" rectangle together. Sew a house 1" x 5" rectangle and a background 1" x 5" rectangle to the top of the unit. Sew a house 1½" x 5" rectangle to the bottom of the unit. Press the

seam allowances as indicated. The right window unit should measure 5" x 4½".

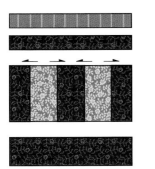

Assembling the Block

1. Sew the left and right window units together. Press the seam allowances toward the left unit. The window section should measure 4½" x 8½".

2. Sew the chimney row, roof row, and window section together to complete the block. Press the seam allowances as indicated. Make 20 blocks.

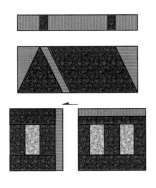

Make 20.

Assembling and Finishing the Quilt

1. Arrange the House blocks in five rows of four blocks each. Place a blue rectangle between the blocks in each row. Sew the blocks and sashing rectangles together to make five rows. Press the seam allowances toward the rectangles.

Make 5.

2. For the sashing rows, lay out four blue rectangles horizontally, alternating them with cream 2" squares. Sew the pieces together. Press the seam allowances toward the rectangles. Repeat to make four sashing rows.

Make 4.

3. Join all rows, starting and ending with a block row. Press the seam allowances toward the sashing rows. The quilt top should measure 37" x 46½".

4. Sew the blue 2½" x 37" strips to the top and bottom of the quilt top. Press the seam allowances toward the blue strips. Join the blue 2½" x 42" strips end to end. From the pieced strip, cut two 50½"-long strips and sew them to the sides of the quilt top. Press the seam allowances toward the border strips.

Quilt assembly

5. Layer the backing, batting, and quilt top. Baste, and then quilt as desired.

6. Using the blue 2¼"-wide strips, make and attach binding.

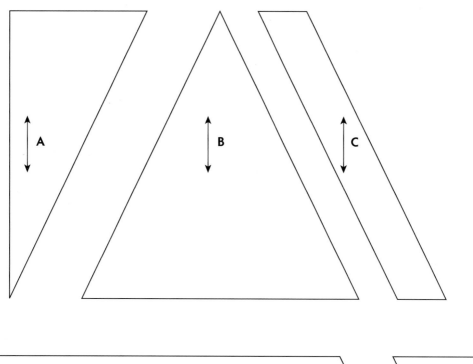

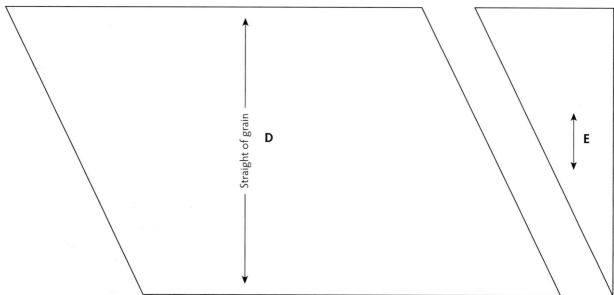

Patterns do not include seam allowances.
Add ¼" seam allowance when cutting fabric pieces.

President's Pride

If you've never tried your hand at a medallion quilt, this is a great opportunity. It's not too big, and most of the blocks are quite easy. Notice, in addition, that a plain border separates each round, giving you the chance to square up the quilt and make sure the following round will fit perfectly. Take your time with the Triangle Square Star in the center, and you'll have a quilt to be proud of.

Quilt size: 36½" x 36½"

Finished blocks: 12" x 12", 3" x 3", and 4½" x 4½"

Materials

Yardage is based on 42"-wide fabric.

⅛ yard *each* of 15 assorted light prints for blocks and triangle border

⅛ yard *each* of 15 assorted dark prints for blocks

⅛ yard *each* of 6 assorted red prints for blocks and triangle border

⅓ yard of dark-blue print for border 4

⅛ yard of beige print for Triangle Square Star block

⅛ yard of medium-blue print for border 2

⅓ yard of brown print for binding

1 yard of fabric for backing

40" x 40" piece of batting

Cutting

Measurements include ¼"-wide seam allowances.

Cutting for Triangle Square Star Block

From *each* of 8 dark prints, cut:

1 square, 3⅞" x 3⅞" (8 total); cut the square in half diagonally to yield 2 triangles (16 total)

From the beige print, cut:

4 squares, 3⅞" x 3⅞"; cut the squares in half diagonally to yield 8 triangles

4 squares, 3½" x 3½"

Cutting for Triangle Border

From the assorted red prints, cut:

12 squares, 2⅞" x 2⅞"; cut the squares in half diagonally to yield 24 triangles

From the assorted light prints, cut:

12 squares, 2⅞" x 2⅞"; cut the squares in half diagonally to yield 24 triangles

From *1* of the light prints, cut:

4 squares, 2½" x 2½"

Continued on page 63

Continued from page 61

Cutting for 1 Nine Patch Block

Cut 28 blocks total.

From *1* of the assorted dark prints, cut:
5 squares, 1½" x 1½"
4 matching squares, 1½" x 1½"

From *1* of the assorted light prints, cut:
5 matching squares, 1½" x 1½"
4 matching squares, 1½" x 1½"

Cutting for 1 Shoofly Block

Cut 28 blocks total. The "shoofly" can be darker or lighter than the background, so the fabrics are listed as "background" and "shoofly." You'll need 28 background fabrics and 28 shoofly fabrics. Refer to the photo on page 61 for guidance with fabric placement as needed.

From *1* of the background fabrics, cut:
2 squares, 2⅜" x 2⅜"; cut the squares in half
    diagonally to yield 4 triangles
4 squares, 2" x 2"

From *1* of the shoofly fabrics, cut:
2 squares, 2⅜" x 2⅜"; cut the squares in half
    diagonally to yield 4 triangles
1 square, 2" x 2"

Cutting for Borders and Binding

From the medium-blue print, cut:
2 strips, 1½" x 16½"
2 strips, 1½" x 18½"

From the dark-blue print, cut:
2 strips, 2" x 24½"
2 strips, 2" x 27½"

From the brown print, cut:
4 strips, 2¼" x 42"

Making the Triangle Square Star Block

1. Sew a beige triangle to a dark 3⅞" triangle to make a half-square-triangle unit. Press the seam allowances toward the dark triangle. Make eight units.

Make 8.

2. Repeat step 1, sewing two different dark 3⅞" triangles together. Press the seam allowances toward the darker triangle. Make four units.

3. Arrange the beige 3½" squares and the units from steps 1 and 2 in four rows as shown, making sure to position units so that the dark triangles form eight star points. Sew the pieces together into rows and press the seam allowances as indicated. Sew the rows together and press the seam allowances in one direction. The block should measure 12½" x 12½".

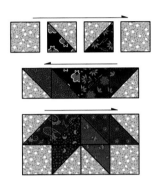 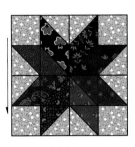

Make 1.

Making the Triangle Border

1. Sew a light 2⅞" triangle to a red 2⅞" triangle to make a half-square-triangle unit. Press the seam allowances toward the red triangle. The unit should measure 2½" x 2½". Make 24 units.

2. Sew six units from step 1 together, orienting the dark triangles as shown. Make two borders for the top and bottom of the quilt center. For the side borders, sew six units together in the same manner, and join a light 2½" square to each end. Make two borders. Press the seam allowances as indicated.

Make 2.

Make 2.

Making the Nine Patch Blocks

Select five matching dark 1½" squares and four matching light 1½" squares. Sew the squares together into rows, pressing the seam allowances toward the darker fabrics. Sew the rows together to make a Nine Patch block. Press the seam allowances in one direction. The block should measure 3½" x 3½". Make 14 blocks.

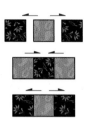

Make 14.

Making the Reverse Nine Patch Blocks

Select five matching light 1½" squares and four matching dark 1½" squares. Sew the squares together into rows, pressing the seam allowances toward the darker fabrics. Sew the rows together to make a reverse Nine Patch block. Press the seam allowances in one direction. The block should measure 3½" x 3½". Make 14 blocks.

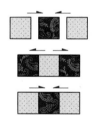

Make 14.

Making the Shoofly Blocks

Use one shoofly fabric and one background fabric for each block. Refer to the photo on page 61 for help with fabric placement as needed.

1. Sew a shoofly 2⅜" triangle to a background 2⅜" triangle to make a half-square-triangle unit. Press the seam allowances toward the darker triangle. The unit should measure 2" x 2". Make four units.

2. Arrange the half-square-triangle units, four background 2" squares, and one shoofly 2" square in three rows. Sew the pieces together into rows, and press the seam allowances as indicated. Sew the rows together. Press. The block should measure 5" x 5". Make 28 blocks.

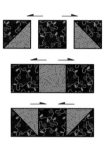

Make 28.

Assembling and Finishing the Quilt

1. Sew the triangle borders to the top, bottom, and sides of the Triangle Square Star block. Press the seam allowances as indicated. The quilt-top center should measure 16½" x 16½".

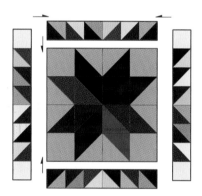

2. Sew the medium-blue 1½" x 16½" strips to the top and bottom of the quilt-top center. Sew the medium-blue 1½" x 18½" strips to the sides of the quilt top. Press all seam allowances toward the medium-blue strips.

3. Sew three Nine Patch blocks and three reverse Nine Patch blocks together to make a border strip. Make two borders for the top and bottom of the quilt. Sew four Nine Patch blocks and four reverse Nine Patch blocks together to make a

border strip. Make two side borders. Press all seam allowances in the same direction.

Make 2.

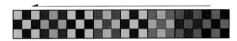

Make 2.

4. Sew the Nine Patch borders to the top, bottom, and sides of the quilt top. Press the seam allowances toward the medium-blue border. The quilt-top center should measure 24½" x 24½".

5. Sew the dark-blue 2" x 24½" strips to the top and bottom of the quilt-top center. Sew the dark-blue 2" x 27½" strips to the sides of the quilt top. Press all seam allowances toward the dark-blue strips.

6. Sew six Shoofly blocks together to make a border strip. Make two borders for the top and bottom of the quilt. Sew eight Shoofly blocks together to make a border strip. Make two side borders. Press all seam allowances in the same direction.

Make 2.

Make 2.

7. Sew the Shoofly borders to the top, bottom, and sides of the quilt top. Press the seam allowances toward the dark-blue border.

8. Layer the backing, batting, and quilt top. Baste, and then quilt as desired.

9. Using the brown 2¼"-wide strips, make and attach binding.

Quilt assembly

Brother Fought Brother

The Star block featured in this handsome quilt was a common component in many Civil War–era quilts. Set with Snowball blocks, the stars form chains that suggest brothers banding together, although we know, tragically, that brothers also battled against one another in the War between the States.

Quilt size: 47" x 55½"
Finished blocks: 6" x 6"

Materials
Yardage is based on 42"-wide fabric.
1⅜ yards of black tone on tone for Snowball blocks and setting triangles
1¼ yards *total* of assorted red and orange prints for blocks and pieced border
⅛ yard *each* of 15 assorted light prints for Star blocks
⅓ yard *total* of assorted black prints for Star blocks
⅓ yard *total* of assorted gold prints for Star blocks
⅓ yard of dark-gold print for Snowball blocks
½ yard of dark small-scale check for binding
3 yards of fabric for backing (pieced horizontally)
51" x 59" piece of batting

Cutting
Measurements include ¼"-wide seam allowances.

From the assorted red and orange prints, cut:
30 sets of 4 matching squares, 2⅜" x 2⅜" (120 total); cut the squares in half diagonally to yield 8 matching triangles (240 total)
45 to 48 pieces, 2½" x various lengths ranging from 2½" to 6½"

From the assorted light prints, cut:
30 sets of 4 matching squares, 2⅜" x 2⅜" (120 total); cut the squares in half diagonally to yield 8 matching triangles (240 total)
30 sets of 4 matching squares, 2" x 2" (120 total)

From the assorted black prints, cut:
30 sets of 2 matching squares, 2⅜" x 2⅜" (60 total); cut the squares in half diagonally to yield 4 matching triangles (120 total)

From the assorted gold prints, cut:
30 sets of 2 matching squares, 2⅜" x 2⅜" (60 total); cut the squares in half diagonally to yield 4 matching triangles (120 total)

Continued on page 68

Continued from page 66

From the black tone on tone, cut:

4 strips, 6½" x 42"; crosscut into 20 squares, 6½" x 6½"

5 squares, 10" x 10"; cut the squares into quarters diagonally to yield 20 side triangles (2 will be left over)*

2 squares, 6" x 6"; cut the squares in half diagonally to yield 4 corner triangles*

From the dark-gold print, cut:

4 strips, 2" x 42"; crosscut into 80 squares, 2" x 2"

From the dark small-scale check, cut:

6 strips, 2¼" x 42"

The side and corner triangles are slightly oversized and will be trimmed later.

Making the Star Blocks

Use one red (or orange) print, one black print, one gold print, and two light prints for each block.

1. Sew a light triangle to a red (or orange) triangle to make a half-square-triangle unit. Press the seam allowances toward the darker triangle. Make eight units.

Make 8.

2. Sew a black triangle to a gold triangle to make a half-square-triangle unit. Press the seam allowances toward the black triangle. Make four units.

Make 4.

3. Arrange four matching light squares and the units from steps 1 and 2 in four rows as shown. Sew the units together into rows and press the seam allowances as indicated. Sew the rows together and press the seam allowances in one direction. The block should measure 6½" x 6½". Make 30 blocks.

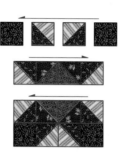 

Make 30.

Making the Snowball Blocks

Draw a diagonal line on the wrong side of four dark-gold 2" squares. Place marked squares on opposite corners of a black 6½" square, right sides together. Sew on the drawn line. Trim the outside corners of the gold squares only, ¼" from the stitched line. Press the seam allowances toward the corners. In the same way, sew gold squares to the remaining two corners of the black square. Make 20 Snowball blocks.

Make 20.

CHANGE IT UP

For a change of pace, use light background prints instead of black for the Snowball blocks and setting triangles. Or, go completely scrappy and don't worry about color placement.

Assembling and Finishing the Quilt

1. Arrange the Star blocks, Snowball blocks, and black side and corner triangles in diagonal rows as shown. Sew the blocks and side triangles into rows. Join the rows and add the corner triangles last. Press the seam allowances as indicated. Trim the oversized triangles all around, leaving an equal amount from the block corners so that the quilt top measures 43" x 51½".

Quilt assembly

2. Randomly sew red and orange 2½"-wide pieces end to end to make a 43"-long strip for the top border. Repeat to make the bottom border. Randomly sew red and orange 2½"-wide pieces end to end to make two 55½"-long strips for the side borders. Press all seam allowances in one direction.

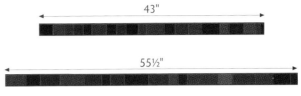

Make 2 of each.

3. Sew the top, bottom, and side borders to the quilt top. Press the seam allowances toward the border strips.

Quilt plan

4. Layer the backing, batting, and quilt top. Baste, and then quilt as desired.

5. Using the dark-check 2¼"-wide strips, make and attach binding.

The Oaks

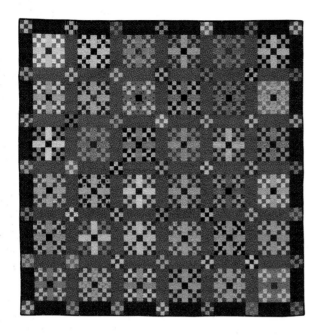

Pieced in the colors of the great oaks that graced estates in the North and South alike, this Nine Patch quilt is both easy to make and easy to live with. It's a generously sized lap quilt that's sure to look inviting draped on your sofa or favorite armchair.

Quilt size: 66½" x 66½"
Finished blocks: 7½" x 7½" and 3" x 3"

Materials

Yardage is based on 42"-wide fabric.
¼ yard *each* of 24 assorted medium or dark prints in red, mustard, brown, green, gold, and orange for blocks
¼ yard *each* of 16 assorted light prints for blocks
1¼ yards of light-rust print for sashing
⅝ yard of dark-rust print for border
½ yard of dark-brown print for binding
4¼ yards of fabric for backing (pieced horizontally)
70" x 70" piece of batting

Cutting

Measurements include ¼"-wide seam allowances.

Cutting for 1 Large Nine Patch Block
Cut 36 blocks total.

From 1 of the medium or dark prints, cut:
20 squares, 1½" x 1½"
1 square, 2" x 2"

From 1 of the assorted light prints, cut:
16 matching squares, 1½" x 1½"
4 matching rectangles, 2" x 3½"

Cutting for 1 Small Nine Patch Block
Cut 49 blocks total.

From 1 of the assorted medium or dark prints, cut:
5 matching squares, 1½" x 1½"

From 1 of the assorted light prints, cut:
4 matching squares, 1½" x 1½"

Cutting for Sashing, Border, and Binding

From the light-rust print, cut:
12 strips, 3½" x 42"; crosscut into 60 rectangles, 3½" x 8"

From the dark-rust print, cut:
3 strips, 3½" x 42"; crosscut into 24 rectangles, 3½" x 8"

From the dark-brown print, cut:
7 strips, 2¼" x 42"

Making the Large Nine Patch Blocks

Use 20 matching dark 1½" squares, 16 matching light 1½" squares, four matching light 2" x 3½" rectangles, and one dark 2" square for each block.

1. Sew five dark and four light 1½" squares together into rows, pressing the seam allowances toward the darker fabrics. Sew the rows together to make an individual Nine Patch block. Press the seam allowances in one direction. The block should measure 3½" x 3½". Make four matching blocks.

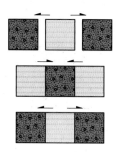

Make 4.

2. Sew the Nine Patch blocks, light rectangles, and dark 2" square together in rows as shown. Press the seam allowances toward the light rectangles. Sew the rows together. Press the seam allowances toward the center. Make 36 blocks.

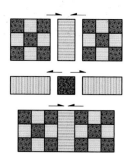
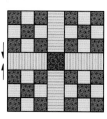

Make 36.

Making the Small Nine Patch Blocks

Use five matching dark 1½" squares and four matching light 1½" squares for each block.

Sew the dark and light squares together into rows, pressing the seam allowances toward the darker fabrics. Sew the rows together to make a Nine Patch block. Press the seam allowances in one direction. The block should measure 3½" x 3½". Make 49 blocks.

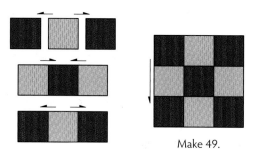

Make 49.

Assembling and Finishing the Quilt

1. Arrange the large Nine Patch blocks in six rows of six blocks each. Place a light-rust rectangle between the blocks in each row, and add dark-rust rectangles on the ends of each row. Sew the blocks and sashing rectangles together to make six rows. Press the seam allowances toward the sashing rectangles.

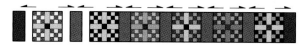

Make 6.

2. For the sashing rows between the block rows, lay out six light-rust rectangles horizontally, alternating them with seven small Nine Patch blocks. Sew the pieces together and press the seam allowances toward the light-rust rectangles. Make five sashing rows.

Make 5.

3. Make the top and bottom border rows using six dark-rust rectangles and seven small Nine Patch blocks. Press the seam allowances toward the dark-rust rectangles.

Make 2.

4. Join all the rows, starting with a dark-rust border row, then alternating the block and sashing rows and ending with the remaining dark-rust border row. Press the seam allowances toward the sashing and border rows.

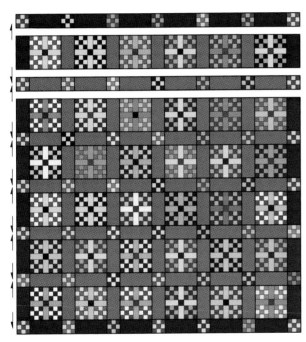

Quilt assembly

5. Layer the backing, batting, and quilt top. Baste, and then quilt as desired.

6. Using the dark-brown 2¼"-wide strips, make and attach binding.

Buckwheat Star

Nothing says "thrift" like string piecing. Make the most of leftover strips or a collection of fat quarters by sewing narrow strips randomly onto foundations to create the star points. The effect is dramatic, and you'll feel good about using up and making do. This is a great quilt to snuggle under, but you can also hang it proudly on the wall to see it in all its glory.

Quilt size: 64½" x 64½"
Finished blocks: 16" x 16" and 4" x 4"

Materials

Yardage is based on 42"-wide fabric. Fat quarters are approximately 18" x 21".

1 fat quarter *each* of 25 assorted light, medium, and dark prints for blocks
1 fat quarter *each* of 9 assorted cream prints for blocks
1⅞ yards of red print for sashing and border
½ yard of dark-blue print for binding
4¼ yards of fabric for backing (pieced horizontally)
68" x 68" piece of batting
Foundation-piecing paper or newspaper

Cutting

Measurements include ¼"-wide seam allowances.

From the assorted light prints, cut:
32 squares, 1½" x 1½"

From the assorted dark prints, cut:
32 squares, 1½" x 1½"

From the remaining assorted prints, cut:
170 to 180 strips, 1" to 1½" x 21"*

From the assorted cream prints, cut:
9 squares, 7⅞" x 7⅞"; cut the squares into quarters diagonally to yield 36 triangles
9 sets of 4 matching squares, 5¼" x 5¼" (36 total)

From the red print, cut:
13 strips, 4½" x 42"; cut *6 of the strips* into 12 rectangles, 4½" x 16½"

From the dark-blue print, cut:
7 strips, 2¼" x 42"

You may want to cut a few strips of each fabric in various widths, and then cut more strips as needed. The number of strips required will depend on their width and how efficiently you use them.

USE SHORT STITCHES!

Before you start string piecing onto the foundation paper, adjust your sewing machine to a very short stitch length. The shorter stitches will perforate the foundation paper more effectively than longer stitches and allow for easier paper removal.

Making the Diamond Units

For complete paper-piecing instructions, visit ShopMartingale.com/HowtoQuilt for free downloadable information.

1. Using the foundation pattern on page 79, trace or photocopy 72 diamonds onto foundation paper or newspaper. If you photocopy the pattern, compare the printed version to the pattern in the book to make sure it's accurate.

2. Place a fabric strip, right side up, in the approximate center of a diamond foundation, making sure the strip extends at least ½" beyond both sides of the paper.

3. Place a second fabric strip on top of the first strip, right sides together and with the long edges aligned. Make sure the second strip extends at least ½" beyond both sides of the paper. Stitch along the long edge of the strips, using a ¼" seam allowance. Press.

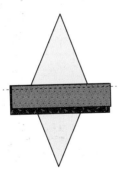

4. Working from the center of the diamond toward each point, continue sewing strips to the foundation paper in the same manner. For added interest, do not line up the strips exactly straight with the previously sewn strip.

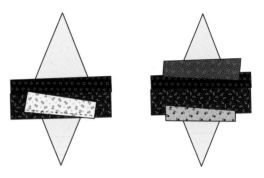

5. When you have completely covered the paper foundation, gently press the diamond unit. Trim the excess fabric ¼" beyond the edge of the paper foundation using a ruler and rotary cutter. Do not remove the paper yet. Make 72 diamond units.

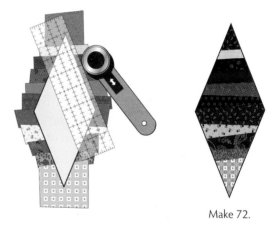

Make 72.

Making the Star Blocks

1. Randomly select two diamond units and place them right sides together. Use pins to match the beginning and ending points on the paper foundation and align the edges of the paper. Pin in place. Starting ¼" from the outer edge of the fabric (exactly at the corner of the paper), backstitch and then stitch along the edge of the

paper, sew the diamonds together to make a quarter-star unit. Press the seam allowances in one direction. Make 36 quarter-star units.

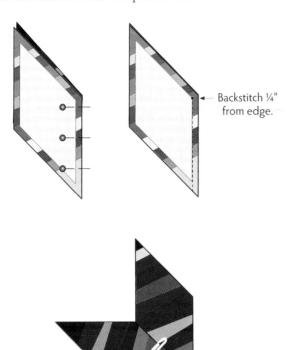

← Backstitch ¼" from edge.

Make 36.

2. Select two quarter-star units and sew them together as instructed in step 1 to make a half-star unit. Press the seam allowances in one direction. Make 18 half-star units.

Make 18.

3. Select two half-star units and sew them together in the same manner to make a star unit. Press. Make nine star units.

Make 9.

4. Select four cream squares and four cream triangles, all matching. Place a cream square on top of a diamond unit, right sides together and raw edges aligned. Sew from the outside raw edge to the inside corner, stopping ¼" from the edge with a backstitch.

Backstitch ¼" from edge.

5. With right sides together, position the second diamond unit on top of the square so that the raw edges are aligned and the point of the star extends beyond the edge of the square as shown. Sew from the outside edge to the inside corner, stopping at the corner of the paper with a backstitch.

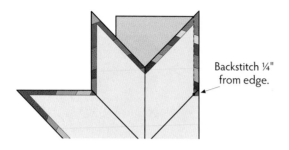

Backstitch ¼"
from edge.

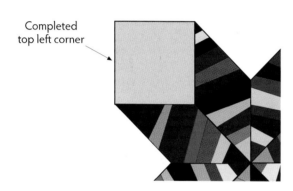

Completed
top left corner

6. Repeat steps 4 and 5, sewing cream squares to the remaining three corners of the star unit. Then sew cream triangles to the sides of the star unit. Press all seam allowances toward the cream squares and triangles. Remove the paper foundations. Make nine Star blocks.

Make 9.

Making the Checkerboard Blocks

1. Randomly select two light and two dark 1½" squares. Sew them together to make a four-patch unit. Press the seam allowances as indicated. Make 16 units.

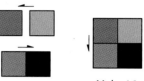

Make 16.

2. Sew four of the assorted four-patch units from step 1 together to make a 16-patch Checkerboard block. Press the seam allowances as indicated. The block should measure 4½" x 4½". Make four blocks.

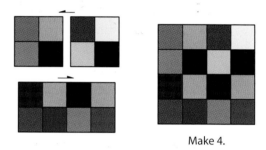

Make 4.

Assembling and Finishing the Quilt

1. Arrange the Star blocks, Checkerboard blocks, and red sashing rectangles in rows, referring to the quilt-assembly diagram on page 79. Join the pieces into rows and press the seam allowances toward the sashing rectangles. Join the rows and press the seam allowances toward the sashing rows. The quilt top should measure 56½" x 56½".

2. Join the remaining red 4½"-wide strips end to end. From the pieced strip, cut two 56½"-long strips and two 64½"-long strips. Sew the 56½"-long strips to the top and bottom of the quilt top. Press the seam allowances toward the red

strips. Sew the 64½"-long strips to the sides
of the quilt top. Press the seam allowances toward
the red strips.

Quilt assembly

3. Layer the backing, batting, and quilt top. Baste,
   and then quilt as desired.
4. Using the dark-blue 2¼"-wide strips, make and
   attach binding.

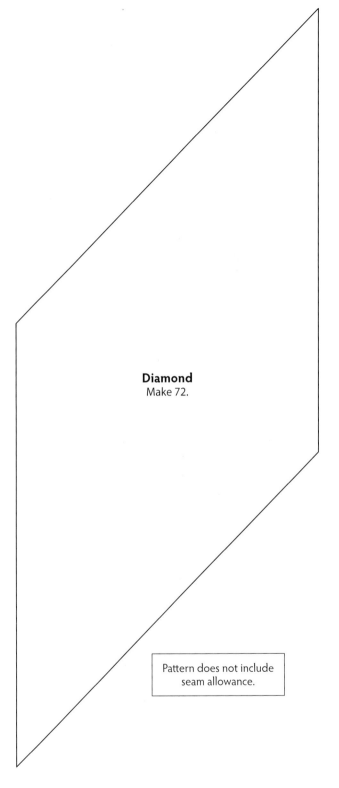

Diamond
Make 72.

Pattern does not include
seam allowance.

About the Authors

Mary and Janey; photo by Susan Henderson

Connie and Lucy; photo by Roy Tesene

Retirement seemed a distant thing in my life until 2014, when Connie and I closed Country Threads Quilt Shop on October 31. After 32 years of sharing my small farm with the public, I can now let all the animals roam free around the yard. I board my friends' and family's dogs when they go out of town and the dogs have the run of seven fenced acres. I plan to add several more dog "rooms" in the quilt shop and make a sewing area for my friends to meet and sew.

Here are a few things on my retirement to-do list:
- Read lots of books—even in the middle of the day!
- Enjoy a nap now and then.
- Go to the local care center and find a new resident to visit.
- Teach my dogs some tricks. I wish they could do agility training.
- Enjoy my garden and yard and all the maintenance that goes along with it.
- Volunteer more at my church.
- Paint some old furniture.
- Visit some antique fairs with Connie.
- Clean, water, and repot all the succulents.
- Go to a movie matinee now and then.
- Go out for lunch with friends.
- Organize my sewing room.

And most of all, I want to sew just for the fun of it—without writing directions and checking yardage to see if we can cut a matching kit.

Oh, it's been a fabulous, wonderful, exciting 32 years, but I know there's a new life waiting just around the corner for both of us.

Mary

Kittens seem to mark important moments in my life! Six years ago, Mary gave me three kittens when I got home from having breast-cancer surgery. I was *very* lucky and just had to have a lumpectomy and radiation. Now, as I'm about to retire and start a new chapter in this old life, we have adopted two kittens from the local humane society. I can hardly wait to watch them grow up. How can life get any better when there are kittens involved?

Mary and I are both looking forward to our retirement. Here are just a few of the things I have on my long list:
- Strip the wallpaper from our living-room walls.
- Paint several rooms.
- Make a quilt for our new bed. The mattresses are so deep that nothing seems to fit.
- Visit our kids and grandkids.
- Read more books.
- Drink more coffee while exploring Pinterest.
- Visit Mary and her dogs and cats.
- Go on long walks with Hope, our black lab.
- Volunteer more at our local library, church, and movie theater.
- Garden.
- Take some cooking classes.
- Continue those *darn* exercise classes.

But most of all, I want to sew. It will be wonderful to just sew—with no deadlines and just for the joy of it! I'm sure you'll find me in my sewing room most days.

I want to thank Martingale for the opportunity of working with them again. You guys are the best!

Connie